Life
from the
Ruins

An Accounting of my Childhood and Youth in Germany and USA

FRITZ JAENSCH

Life from the Ruins

iUniverse books may be ordered through booksellers or by contacting:

iUniverse
1663 Liberty Drive
Bloomington, IN 47403
www.iuniverse.com
1-800-Authors (1-800-288-4677)

Because of the dynamic nature of the Internet, any web addresses or links contained in this book may have changed since publication and may no longer be valid. The views expressed in this work are solely those of the author and do not necessarily reflect the views of the publisher, and the publisher hereby disclaims any responsibility for them.

Any people depicted in stock imagery provided by Getty Images are models, and such images are being used for illustrative purposes only. Certain stock imagery © Getty Images.

ISBN: 978-1-5320-9168-1 (sc)
ISBN: 978-1-5320-9169-8 (e)

Library of Congress Control Number: 2020905783

Print information available on the last page.

iUniverse rev. date: 03/27/2020

1

◆

A Letter of Introduction

Dear daughter Marianne:

When last we met, you asked me to write—for the benefit of your sons—a history of their roots in Germany to equal their roots in the American Cherokee Nation. I'll tell you what I shall do, dear girl. I shall write what I know and remember in letters to you. How is that? We can then share that with the rest of the family.

Since you are the one who asked me, I might as well begin my history of our family with you, Marianne Esther. I wonder if you even remember your middle name, Esther. It was my wish that you have that middle name. Not long before your birth in San Francisco's Kaiser Hospital, your sister, Elke, your brother, Chris, your mom, and I went to see the movie *Esther*. It was the story of the Jewish girl, niece of wise Mordecai, who became the wife of the Persian king Ahasuerus. Queen Esther's courage saved her people against formidable odds. You, Marianne, do well living up to that name. Your strong integrity has pulled you and your loved ones through many dangers.

Your first name, Marianne, is the name of your grandmother: Marianne Karschewski. She married Hermann Sagurski. They lived in the Rhineland of Germany before they moved to the region called Pommern, and that is where your grandfather Hermann managed a farm. From Pommern, they moved to East Prussia in the Baltics, the Polish part of Germany. That's where we all are from.

Marianne and Hermann Sagurski had four daughters. Their firstborn was your aunt Gertrude. Elke and her cousin Gudrun called her "Date." Everybody did when I got to know Elke and your mom, who both lived with her then. Elke's middle name is Gertrude after her and your aunt. The second Sagurski daughter is your aunt Else. She and her husband, Heini, settled in East Germany after the Great War. I am sad that I was never able to meet them. Omi, your grandma, knew them well. The third Sagurski girl is your aunt Waltraud, Gudrun's mother. Your mother, Klara, is the youngest of Marianne Sagurski's children. Your mother and I met and married in Worms on the Rhine River when I was stationed there as a GI in the United States Army.

Marianne Morris, née Jaensch, with Michael Brian, her firstborn

Chris

Marianne

Elke, Marianne, and Chris

Elke and Fritz/Dad

Your mother's childhood and mine were parallel in some respects. Both of us lived on farms in eastern Germany during the Second World War, and both of us had to flee the advancing victorious Red Army. But your mother's childhood was far more perilous. As that war drew to a close, in the fall of 1944 and spring of 1945, your grandmother Marianne was left with her four daughters in the city of Stralsund at the Baltic Sea coast. While the Russian army approached, shooting the city into a heap of rubble, your grandmother and her children got away "by the skin of their teeth" on a leaky ship to Denmark.

In Denmark, in a refugee camp, your grandmother underwent a gallbladder operation. Today, that procedure is quite simple, but at that time, the doctor could not prevent a blood clot from forming. The clot stopped Marianne Sagurski's heart. I knew her only from what your mom and your aunties told me about her life. She died in 1945 in Denmark, and you inherited her name.

Years later, in 1953, after I had learned the farmworker's trade, I also went to Denmark. I was an exchange student and worked on a farm called Brondstruplund on the island of Fyn. On that island is the town called Odense, the birthplace of Hans Christian Andersen. When I visited the little cottage where that teller of beautiful stories was born, I was deeply impressed. I came away with a heartfelt wish that, should I ever father a son, his name would be Hans Christian, called Chris. That is how your brother got his name.

Next, I shall relate something about the Second World War, and us Germans in it, since I have already mentioned it. Many books have been written about that conflagration. Some historians say that it was the last righteous war where everybody knew what side they were on. I subscribe to that assessment, at least so far as Europe is concerned, where the war was started by Germany. I'll take a little time to think about how I shall defend that point of view—and how I shall place our family's story in it.

A Thought Interlude

Walk into any library, and you can easily get discouraged. Ranks and ranks of books on shelves contain the wisdom of the rising and falling and rising generations of humankind. It is as if the voice of wisdom says, "Every ambition, every joy and sorrow, all the great works and tragic defeats of the human heart and the human endeavor on earth—all of the emotions from the high-minded and spiritual down to the vulgar and pornographic—are on these shelves. And you want to write yet one more book?"

Hardly anyone looks at books anymore. Humanity is undergoing an intellectual revolution: cyberspace. With the invention and use of electronic thinking machines, fingers on keys make visible the entire scale of human experience in a flash.

Books? Who will take the time to read them tomorrow? The time might well come when people congratulate each other for doing away with the need for paper, thus saving the planet from the destruction of forests in paper mills. There might be no more letter-writing a few years hence, no more post offices to convey the freight of paper-borne messages from longing hearts and minds to longing hearts—or from stern debt collectors to poor debtors, unable to pay. The big office silos in the cities might well empty out. The crowded freeways will make way for weeds that push through the crumbling concrete. People will hole up in caves behind the keyboards of their computers. All the books of the world will come to their screens. All their needs and wants will come to them on the screen.

Of course, the whole thing can easily collapse for lack of maintenance or in the course of cyber wars for control of the satellites and relay stations. Humans, after all, have yet to learn to live in peace with each other in the world that surrounds them. No matter how sophisticated we get, the model of success is still to "get there firstest with the mostest," football-like block, block, block, and run them down. Wait until the guy looks away—and then sneak in and take what he thinks is his. The world loves a winner. Football business, football politics, football medicine, football justice, and football religion are the basic instincts we have yet to overcome.

The vanquished ones—from that proud march of power—leave little behind from which to reconstruct what might have been their joys and sorrows, but they were human, very much like those who overwhelmed them. Therefore, some of who they were and what they thought was likely absorbed and integrated into the thoughts, habits, and works of the victorious civilizations in their time. The historian tries to search and sort it all out to see how we got from there to here and to see what of value we might have overlooked in the heat of the game or thrown away as trash between the bleachers.

You see, the march of time is not synonymous with progress. Progress is an increase of love and peace among us! Can you imagine love as integral part of daily life, work, and planning? Do!

January 2, 1997

Dear Marianne:

This morning, I thought about how to continue my story of our German roots. For a moment, the seeming futility of such an endeavor overran my mind. The accompanying paper was the result. I send it along to you because the paper demonstrates an initial obstacle faced at the beginning of every worthy endeavor—an obstacle that can, and must, be overcome.

It's true that all of what we set out to do is probably done easier and equally as well or better by many other people. Nevertheless, the field for the human endeavor is thereby not diminished. Your work is as valuable as the next person's, and the field for our labor is certainly still there. In our case, it consists of an effort to understand and tell what happened where our forebears and ancestors lived. Ours is an effort to seek out whatever was noble and good in their living so that we can avail ourselves of that and build on it.

So where were we? Oh, yes. I wanted to explain World War II, the event that made your mother's family, as well as mine, refugees and how in time, looking westward, we found our work and livelihood here in the United States of America. Let me first tell you a little about East Prussia, the Baltic region our family called home when I was a child.

Wars of conquest did not begin with Spain's and England's invasions of America. European native populations suffered such conquests with every bit as much pain and loss of life and cultural heritage as did Native American people. When I started school in Königsberg in East Prussia, I liked that part of social studies called *Heimatkunde*, or information about the history of our home region.

I especially enjoyed the story of a decisive thirteenth-century battle that pitted the Germanic Knights of the Cross and their fellow colonizers against the "Pruzzi," the native people of that region, from whom Prussia took its name. The battle apparently went back and forth across the Pregel River. All battles in those days were hand-to-hand combat. In that kind of warfare, the opposing forces depended on the battle standard to rally around and know who was friend or foe. At one point in the battle, the Pruzzi managed to bring down the standard of the German Knights. A shoemaker stuck his shoe on a javelin for a flag and prevented confusion among the German forces. They won the victory. Nothing remained of the Pruzzi but the name they gave to that region of Germany, which eventually stretched from Baltic East Prussia all the way to the Rhine River and the city of Cologne.

How much of the blood of those vanquished native Pruzzi, or their neighbors, the Kuren is still in us? Who knows? Some of the Kuren people survive to the present day in fishing villages, such as the one called Nidden at the banks of the Kuren Lagoon and the Baltic Sea. Your grandmother told me that people in Nidden still spoke their ancient native language in our time. They also plied the waters of the lagoon with their fishing barges.

I have expanded a little on this ancient story because the fate of the old Prussians is something Native Americans can identify with. The Order of the Knights of the Cross was formed by Emperor Frederic of Hohenstaufen in the twelfth century to guard the trade routes and pilgrim routes to Jerusalem.

KURENFISCHEREI

Für das Kurische Haff, dieses fischreichste Gewässer Deutschlands, waren die schweren, schwarzgeteerten Kurenkähne (links unten) mit ihren bunten Wimpeln (links oben) besonders charakteristisch. Einzeln oder zu zweit betrieben sie nachts die Schleppnetzfischerei, und vor allem im Frühjahr und im Herbst brachten sie reiche Fänge — Fische aller Sorten: Zander, Hechte, Brassen, Barsche, Schnäpel, Aale, Quappen — an Land.

Kurenfischerei

Fur das Kurische Haff, dieses fischreichste Gewasser Deutschlands, waren die schweren, schwarzgeteerten Kurenkahne (links unten) mit thren bunten Wimpeln (links oben) besonders charakteristisch. Einzeln oder zu zweit betrieben sie nachts die Schleppnetzfischerei, und vor allem im Fruhjabr und im Herbst brachten sie reiche Fange––Fische aller Sorten: Zander, Hechte, Brassen, Barsche, Schnapel, Aale, Quappen—an Land.

When those forces were not needed for that task, the emperor redeployed them to expand the Holy Roman Empire eastward into the Baltic regions. Subduing the people who lived on the land, the forces known as the Knights of the Cross settled the region with Germans. Eventually, their eastward march was halted by a band of Russian warriors under the command of Alexander Nevsky. They lured the heavily armored knights on horseback onto the icy lake, and when it broke, they drowned.

However, the city of Königsberg and the region around it remained theirs. That city and the East Prussian region around it has always been of strategic importance. The shipping lanes to the city could be kept open in winter. That made Königsberg an ideal port for the grain trade of that fruitful region. Eventually, a university was founded in Königsberg, and that opened the city to the exchange of ideas, thoughts, research, and learning between Russia and the peoples of the West.

That was the good thing, but there was a bad thing too. Wars, lots of them, went back and forth across the frontiers. Most were fought over control of territory. The biggest nations around there were Russia, Austria, and Prussia. Poland, in the middle, was constantly attacked and partitioned among the big three. To the north and east of East Prussia were the Baltic countries of Lithuania, Latvia, and Estonia. They existed most of the time as parts of the Russian Empire. For a significant time, Lithuania was a part of Poland—before it reverted to the status of Russian dependency.

Among the reasons for war, the predominant one was economic. A rich country with a good harbor was worth a fight. But there were other, more volatile reasons for warfare in that region. Predominant among them were ethnicity and religion. Poland was Roman Catholic, and Russia was Greek Orthodox. Whatever other reasons they had to quarrel, religion became the motor of their wars.

During the Reformation in the fifteenth and sixteenth centuries, Prussia—roughly from the Elbe River eastward—became Lutheran. No Germany was yet in existence during the Reformation. Prussia was a part of a multitude of semiautonomous kingdoms, counties, and duchies held together under the Habsburg crown of the Holy Roman Empire. In time, the largest kingdoms of that empire—notably England, Spain, and France, and to a lesser degree, Prussia, Austria, and Italy—settled into nation-states, while Germany was still a region of principalities engaged in trade as well as in warfare. In all those wars, especially the Thirty Years' War (1618–1648), religion played an often-decisive role. It is a fascinating tale this ferment of nations and ideologies in Europe until finally the people were settled into nations with their borders and identities.

In the midst of all this, the parents of the Christian religion, the Jewish people, were living a precarious existence among us. Tolerated—and their marvelous learning and well-trained talents used to the benefit of many a monarch—they were more often grievously harassed, oppressed, and persecuted.

For a time, the eastern parts of Europe, notably Poland and parts of the Ukraine, were more tolerant of Jewish communities that settled there. *The Fiddler on the Roof* and Eli Wiesel's *Souls on Fire* are my favorite descriptions of Jewish life in those regions.

The incomprehensibly deadly persecution we German people visited upon the Jewish people during the so-called Third Reich has burdened my sense of responsibility for my entire life.

Königsberg, Preußen (drawn from memory by Wilhelm Jaensch)

Dear Marianne:

In my last letter, I tried to explain how, in centuries of struggle and wars, Europe evolved into a continent of nation-states with more or less hostility toward each other. Germany was one of the last countries in Europe to come together as a unified nation-state in 1871 in the course of a war against France. From that point onward, the German Empire—with the kaiser (the emperor) as head of government—grew very strong and proud.

As a culture with a unified language, and with art, literature, music, and science to go with that language, Germany was quite old and mature. However, as a political unit with a kaiser and a chancellor on top, Germany was still quite young at the beginning of the twentieth century. You might say that, as a culture, Germany was a wise old sinner who had gone through many ethical ups and downs, learning his lessons as he went. On the whole, the country and its people had made some fine contributions for the good of humankind.

As a political and diplomatic unit, at the turn of the nineteenth to the twentieth century, Germany's behavior resembled that of a teenager in the family of nations. The kaiser, his cabinet, and most politicians threw their weight around and bragged about their invincibility—and most of the people cheered. Your great-grandmother Helene, for example, felt and expressed all her life a childlike devotion to the kaiser. All the while, all the countries of Europe prepared their armies for war, marching and maneuvering all over the place and making secret pacts with each other behind each other's backs. (For detailed descriptions of those developments, take a look at Barbara Tuchman's *The Proud Tower* and *The Guns of August*.) The proud and belligerent behavior of Europe's nations led to the outbreak of World War I in 1914.

I characterized Germany's culture as that of a wise old sinner, and this what I meant. There is, of course, hardly a tribe, nation, or individual on the face of our earth who does not have any scrapes with sin. Sin is a religious term. The meaning of it is rebellion against God. It is given to us to understand God as the spirit that is and the spirit that creates, permeates, and supports life and all life's attributes.

Love, beauty, creativity, peace in the heart, and harmony are among all forms of creation, but sin destroys all life and sucks the life energy out of living forms and beings. Sin uses that energy to build up glamorous structures of power that are based on fear, pride, and morbid fascination. Germany, as a people and as a nation, fell into that trap of death worse than any other people. We Germans are heirs to that disaster and do well to explain it to ourselves.

Bear with me, my daughter. You might find me too long-winded with all my explanations of German culture versus German politics and diplomacy, but all this is important before we can place our family into all these events. The predominant flaw that brought about the First World War was militant nationalism.

At the time, another movement was abroad and growing in strength: international socialism. That movement and its leaders hoped the working-class people in all countries would refuse to fight a war against each other for the profit of the factory owners. Jack London, the American socialist author, belonged to those who had confidence that the workers' solidarity would overrule patriotism and cause the workers to refuse to fight. That did not happen. On the contrary, people went to war jubilantly, albeit not for love of their employers, but for the love of kaiser, king, and country. I believe we can call the First World War a failure and a breakdown of Europe's politics and diplomacy.

After the nations of Europe and America were done butchering each other, Germany was accused of starting it all and made to pay reparations. The Germans turned around and accused the civilian population of boycotting the solders at the front. This so-called stab-in-the-back legend became a ready-made tool in the hands of extremist movements like the National Socialists under Hitler's leadership. They turned that carousel of accusations around once more as they stirred up the existing anti-Semitism into a deadly hatred of the Jewish people in their midst.

At first laughed to scorn by Germany's liberals, that party of Nazis—as Hitler's followers were called by their opponents—gained enough confidence to foment a coup against the government of Bavaria. That coup was put down. The leader, Adolph Hitler, was arrested and put for a time into *Festungshaft* (honorable confinement). He used that time to formulate his racist ideology as the program for his anti-Semitic movement. That program was published as *Mein Kampf*. Few people read that diatribe, and even fewer took its threats seriously.

With the accusation of Jewish internationalism, the Nazis touched a very deep-seated European prejudice. Jewish people, dispersed all over Christian Europe and beyond since the times of the Roman Empire, were severely persecuted throughout those centuries. They had no country, but they had their strong faith. Rallying around the Torah, their sacred law book, their communities were forced to live in designated areas that were called ghettos.

Set apart and unable to join craftsmen's guilds and associations, people of Jewish faith found themselves severely restricted in the work they were allowed to do to make a living. However, in the fields open to their endeavors, Jewish families and communities excelled. Among those fields were medicine, law, the sciences, literary scholarship, trade, and finance. Jewish communities extended and communicated across national boundaries, especially in financial markets, and that skill tended to cause suspicion and jealousy among the people as well as among the nobles who ruled them. These jealousies and suspicions, mixed with all sorts of irrational stereotyping and superstitions, became so ingrained in European consciousness as anti-Semitism that they became a part of Europe's culture. It was a long and complex trail of tears.

Hitler tapped into that dark undercurrent of resentment. When Germany experienced bad times after the defeat in World War I, Hitler built up the Nazi movement based on the most vulgar resentments and prejudices Germans held against the Jewish people in their midst. During the rising of the Hitler crisis, there were no longer any ghettos in Germany. During the Stein/Hardenberg Reforms of the early nineteenth century, Jewish citizens were emancipated, and they lived among the people with all rights conferred on them as subjects and citizens.

The emancipation, however, enhanced rather than abated anti-Semitic jealousies. They kept festering in the minds of the people in the complex web of social strata. Hitler had an uncanny feeling for the potency of that dormant resentment. He knew how to fan it into flames the normal middle-class people were not equipped to put out. Most Germans first either ignored or made fun of Hitler's vulgar tirades. Socialists and Communists understood the danger of the violent challenge from the National Socialists, but they were handicapped. For lack of support from center-left parties and crises in their own ranks, they were unable to overcome the Nazi challenge.

The day came in 1932 when Hitler managed to assemble a parliamentary coalition that made him Germany's chancellor. With that power gained, he led the German nation into a crusade of murderous conquest—the Second World War—until the entire German civilization was reduced to rubble and ruin in May 1945.

Into that time, your mother's and my generation was born. During that horrendous war, we lived our childhoods.

What I have written so far is like going with fast skates on thin ice over a very deep lake. In the depth of that lake of history, there are very complex, intertwined stories of human, social, and spiritual developments. I hope to bring up some of these stories in an effort to explain how our family fared in all that tumult.

Wilhelm and Jlella Jaensch, Johanna's and my parents

Steinstr. 17a.

Blick aus dem fenster der Wohnstube.

Our home in Königsberg (drawn by my father during his time as a prisoner of war in Nuremberg)

2

CHAPTER

Life from the Ruins

In October 1939, the doorbell rang in Steinstrasse 17a in Königsberg in the German province of East Prussia. My mother went to answer the door.

Two men in civilian clothing stood in the entrance and asked, "Are you Hella Jaensch, née Riebensahm?"

When she told them that she was the woman, they identified themselves as agents of the secret police called *Geheime Staatspolizei*, which was better known as the gestapo. They informed her that she was under arrest, but they "were friendly enough," as my mother later told me, to give her time to see that her children were safe in her absence. My mother nursed, diapered, and bedded down my little sister, Johanna, born on May 1, 1939. She sent me off to the grocer, Mr. Wolluschkat, to buy five pounds of potatoes. Although only five years old, I accomplished that errand alone. Normally, my grandmother Helene would have gone with me, but she stayed with my sister. When I came home, my mother was gone. My grandmother, whose home we shared, was alone with us, awaiting my father's return from work.

My father, Wilhelm, was an unemployed artist and Bauhaus scholar. He had taken his family from Frankfurt/Main, the city of my birth, to Königsberg, and gained employment as a city policeman. It was,

I believe, close to the time of my mother's arrest when he learned that all policemen who were drafted into the armed forces, as my father soon was, were transferred into SS units. My father did not join the SS, but he did end up in it anyway. For the time being, however, he continued his work as a city cop in Königsberg.

When my father came home to the news of my mother's arrest, his first priority was the safety of his children. He knew that it would only be a matter of time before he would be drafted. His mother, in whose home we lived, was not able to care for us by herself. Years later, my father explained to me that most of all, he wanted to prevent my sister and me from becoming wards of the state—and he wanted to preserve for us the heritage and closeness of our mother's family, the Riebensahms.

Father went to gestapo headquarters and inquired how long my mother's absence would last. He was informed that she would never be released—and he was strongly advised to divorce her, lest he be implicated by association. Father complied, with his children in mind. It was a decision that, while forgiving him, my mother never accepted. She pointed to Kurt Wieck, the concert violinist, who steadfastly refused to divorce his Jewish wife, despite their estranged relationship, saving her and their son from certain death.[*]

Every person is led to the moment of truth—most often unprepared—and so were my parents. I am not here to judge. I am only observing that the disintegration of my parents' family order was caused by Hitler, who caused the disintegration of the German state. My mother became a victim by Hitler's decree, and my father became a perpetrator by that same decree.

> A thousand may fall at your side,
> ten thousand at your right hand;
> but it will not come near you.

These lines from Psalm 91 return to my mind ever and anon as I search for an understanding of my life. I have walked through a landscape laid waste in the clashing of titans, filled with millions of corpses crushed by "the car of Jagannath," the Hindu symbol of the life force that inexorably advances the lives of all on board, but crushes all who oppose it beneath its wheels. A whole civilization, brutalized and stripped of human decency and dignity, came crashing down around me in rubble and smoke.

But I lived a happy, guarded life, which in retrospect, appears quite miraculous to me.

---

[*] Michael Wieck, *Zeugnis vom Untergang Königsbergs* (Heidelberg: Verlag Lambert Schneider, 1988).

My mother was arrested and thrown in prison because she had helped her school friend, Hannah Arendt, and some other Jewish friends from the Socialist Labor Movement in their escape. Mother had in her passport the record of money transfers to her friends in France and Spain. She also had made a trip to Barcelona, Spain, early in 1934 when I was already on the way. A small inheritance had made that possible.

Since the money was not enough for both of my parents to go, Mother went alone; that was my parents' decision. People in Germany at that time had little confidence in savings banks. She went to Barcelona to see for herself, I believe, the unfolding of socialist Spain. That trip, of course, was also evident in her passport.

Late in 1939, after the start of World War II, a friend of my mother's early years, Dr. Pappenheim, a union organizer, left Paris, where he had fled to ahead of the German army, for Barcelona. He carelessly left behind in Paris a letter sent to him by a mutual friend, Mr. Buske, a pharmacist, who inquired, among others, about "Hella." He had not given her last name, but he had wondered where she might be since she had dropped her active political work a number of years earlier. Gestapo agents, in Paris ahead of the German army, found the letter and arrested Mr. Buske, and he gave away my mother's identity. The gestapo apparently believed that my mother must be a contact person for the resistance. That prompted her arrest.

My mother was an idealist. In her youth, she was active in the Socialist Youth Movement, which struck out in a new direction, hoping to bring about the liberation of the working class. She and her friends read Ossietzky's *Die Weltbühne*, Tucholsky, and other contributors to that journal. They were much, and justifiably, impressed by the works of Käthe Kollwitz and Ernst Barlach. But that empathy with "the proletariat" was in time usurped. Newly revolutionized Russia was the mecca of young socialists in the 1920s. And Russia under Lenin's leadership, in time, albeit not at first, exploited the young idealists' empathy for its own national aggrandizement.

My mother's development along these lines was a gradual one. Hannah Arendt, her onetime schoolmate and lifelong friend, told me in later years how at first my mother's thinking appeared to her hopelessly bourgeois and ineffectively liberal for lack of active political involvement in the workers' cause. After an absence of a number of years, the two friends met again. Hannah Arendt was an accomplished philosopher, and my mother was a learned librarian. My mother—with her faith in the Russian Revolution—had, in Hannah's opinion, become one of Lenin's "useful idiots."

Hannah Arendt saw the need to apply the brakes to Mother's romantic idealism. She pointed out the betrayal of the working class then under way through Moscow's directives––a situation quite evident to her, but not yet to Mother. The convincing warnings of my mother's friend prompted my mother to drop of all further political activism. However, her sympathies continued with the plight of the working class.

Years later, when I immigrated to the United States, my mother sent me off with predictions that my sympathies would be with America's African American people—just as hers had been with the European workers. While that prophecy was correct in principle, I learned upon arrival that I knew next to nothing of the history of American race relations. I had everything to learn before I could hope to find a useful life-promoting place within that saga.

I never asked my mother in-depth questions about the political activism of her young years. I have always been more concerned with my commitment as a Christian and the consequent responsibility to God—rather than to a political party or movement— for my thought and conduct and for what had been done in my name as a German in particular and a human being in principle. And inasmuch as my mother is no longer alive, I cannot ask her now. I can only deduce vaguely, from friends of hers I knew, that her political affiliation must have been radically Socialist and in the union movement.

There were Heinrich and Ida Koch. Aunt Ida often took care of me in my infancy in Frankfurt. Heinrich was master mechanic, trade school instructor, union member, and Socialist. After the war, he founded a commercial laundry in Frankfurt/Main, where I worked before my farm apprenticeship.

Heinz Lang and his wife, whom I met after the war in Halle, were also Socialists from their youth and friends of Mother's from her years in Frankfurt in the 1920s.

Another friend of Mother's, Alex Nickel, was a Communist. He was imprisoned in Buchenwald concentration camp throughout the duration of the war and during Hitler's Third Reich. I made his acquaintance after the war in Frankfurt/Main, where he worked for the American Central Intelligence Agency.

Max Fuerst was a carpenter by trade, a Socialist, and a leader and organizer in the Jewish youth movement. His wife was Margot. Their life story was published in German—and translated but not yet published in English.* Margot was secretary for Hans Litten, the attorney who succeeded in putting Hitler on the witness stand in a court of law. He forced Hitler to admit that he was personally responsible for the lawless acts of his storm troopers, the street gangs known as the SA. Hans Litten paid for his bravery with his life at the hands of that very SA.

These friends were the company my mother kept, and with them, she shared her commitment to social justice. There was one other friend she told me of, Hanne Zander—a socialist youth leader—who became a committed Nazi. Mother met him by chance after she had been released from prison. In answer to her joyful greeting, he only raised his hand silently in a Hitler salute and walked away.

---

* Max Fuerst, *Talisman Scheherezade. Die Schwierigen Zwanziger Jahre* (Munich: DTV, 1978).

3
CHAPTER
Where and How My Parents Met

My mother told me that she and my father met at her parent's home in Hardenberg Straße, about three blocks from where my father lived with his widowed mother. A large circle of talented family members and friends often gathered at my mother's home for house concerts, poetry readings, and drama productions. Two friends, Werner Ostendorf and Horst Ladendorf, once brought along a keen-eyed art student, Wilhelm Jaensch, who had a special talent for drawing caricatures. Although that talent made my mother feel uneasy, she nevertheless did fall in love with Wilhelm.

My mother's family—Riebensahm from her father's side and Schusterus on her mother's side—was a large and many-branched clan of landowners and intellectuals. They were not the famous Junkers, and they were not of nobility. They belonged to the bourgeois middle class, who in the course of the nineteenth century had purchased their land or else had become professionals or civil servants by way of a university education.

Mother was the offspring of the liberal branch of that family. Among the many anecdotes of past family members, there was one she was especially fond of telling. Her grandfather, on her mother's side, apparently annoyed his professors at the University of Berlin with his anti-orthodox activities as a member of the Burschenschaft fraternity. He was bid to leave the school, which he did. He returned to oversee his parents' farm in East Prussia, and in time, he annoyed another pillar of society. This time, it was the Lutheran pastor, whom he confounded by choosing names for his children that could not be found in the church calendar. He educated his children at home, in the liberal tradition, which led to an infatuation with Greek mythology and a love for music and the arts. His daughter Herta and her husband, my mother's parents, had established themselves in the provincial capital and harbor city of Königsberg as partners in a feed and grain business. My mother, Hella, was the oldest of their children. She attended a private lyceum, which was where she met Hannah Arendt. Hannah was already far ahead of her, and— challenging the Abitur exam—was soon gone from that school to university. My mother stayed close to the Arendt family and her friends from the socialist youth movement. She was later apprenticed as a bookseller and librarian, which became her lifelong vocation.

Mother had two brothers. The older of the two, Hans Erich, devoted his life to music. He left home at age fifteen for Berlin, and he studied the piano with Arthur Schnabel. Refusing a stipend offered him by a well-to-do uncle, he financed his studies and his living expenses by playing in the movie houses. That is where, among others, he met and made music with the cellist Gregor Piatigorsky, newly fled from revolutionary Russia. Piatigorsky was four years older than Hans Erich. One day, when they finished accompanying one of the movies, Gregor Piatigorsky turned to him and said, "Riebensahm! Was wissen sie von den Weibern?" (What do you know about the wenches?) My uncle admitted that his knowledge in that field was wanting. For the time being, he had postponed the pursuit of ladies. He also had distanced himself from his family—all for the pursuit of excellence in his discipline. Soon, he was, like his admired teacher, an accomplished and sought-after concert pianist and interpreter, especially of Beethoven's works.

My mother loved her brother very deeply and felt hurt by his coolness toward her. However, she little knew that that aloofness was the price for his later fame, which, in turn, was to save her life.

Mother's youngest brother, Helmuth, grew up to love the soil and growing things. He learned gardening, but in the war, he was drafted into the navy and stationed with the coastal defense batteries in Normandy. He survived the entire retreat through France after D-Day. Captured by French forces at war's end, he died of dysentery. Mother told me I resembled him most of all my relatives with my love for the land and my slow but thorough intellectual grasp of things.

My father came from a family of soldiers and teachers. His mother's ancestors, Austrian Protestants, had migrated away from persecution in their home region and settled in East Prussia. My great grandfather Feller was a soldier, serving as master tailor in a regiment of dragoons in Tilsit. His daughter Helene married my grandfather Arthur Jaensch in 1900.

My grandfather Arthur Jaensch was one of twelve children of a village teacher and his wife, Louise, in Sensburg County in the Masurian region of East Prussia (now Poland). He was a professional soldier, an infantry sergeant, until three years after his marriage. Thereafter, until the outbreak of World War I, he worked as a law clerk. During the war, until his death in 1919, he was a soldier in the quartermaster corps.

My grandparents tried to provide my father with a higher education and enrolled him in the gymnasium in Königsberg. Father later told me that he found himself in a fairly hopeless position as the son of a minor noncommissioned officer in a highly class-conscious elite institution. He lacked intellectual genius in the fields of mathematics, physical sciences, and classical languages. His talents were in art and design and the humanities, which were of secondary importance in that school. At the age of seventeen, Father was forced to leave school. He tried his hand at various vocations: cabinetmaker, clerk in a merchant house, and finally the Staedel School of art in Frankfurt and the Bauhaus school in its last years in Berlin.

When my parents married, both of their fathers were no longer alive. My father's mother—the only grandmother I have known—was left destitute because of her husband's heavy indebtedness. She had to move out of her modestly upscale apartment, and my father found a less expensive, but comfortable flat for her in a cooperative housing development in the Steinstraße. He furnished it with furniture he built from wooden crates he got cheaply at the waterfront and fashioned mattresses for the beds with wood shavings covered with gunnysack material that he dyed blue. I remember it well because my parents lived in my grandma's home when they returned from Frankfurt in my second year of life.

By that time, my mother's mother was no longer alive. The feed and grain business, Riebensahm & Bieler, had gone bankrupt in the Great Depression, and my mother's childhood home was lost.

My father developed two principles during his youth and education: an aversion to indebtedness and a distaste for political involvement. His aversion to debt resulted from his father's early death at the end of World War I. Father, then eighteen, was faced with the fact that my grandfather's drinking habit had put him at the mercy of loan sharks. My father was forced to persuade his mother to sell all her livelihood to pay off those loans. Thereafter, until his life's end, he would live austerely rather than incur any debt. My parents' attempt at operating a photography studio, for which Father was well trained at art school, failed largely because of Father's insistence on operating without the help of credit.

My father's aversion to political activism derived from an experience he had when he was a student at the Bauhaus School of Art in the early thirties. The student body was a reflection of the German body politique as a whole: hopelessly cleft between the various factions of Socialists and Communists on the left, Conservatives, the likes of the "Steel Helmet" organization, and the Nazis on the right. They faced each other belligerently, and the myriad more or less liberal or conservative moderates became ever more ineffective—and their constituents ever more tired of the constantly reoccurring elections. On one occasion, some Communist fellow students of his invited him to participate in a street demonstration. Father went along, swung the banners and shouted along. The next day at school, his friends from the other side of the spectrum demonstratively turned their backs on him. That did it for him. Rather than learning what the aim of the demonstration had been in which he had participated—in order to decide if he could conscientiously endorse it and commit himself to it—he foreswore political involvement altogether. Henceforth, he immersed himself in the discipline of his art, and only through the métier of his art did he express his observations of people around him and their mind-sets and characters.

In retrospect, I believe my father's reaction to his early exposure to the increasingly brutal political confrontations was rather typical for the majority of Germans. Withdrawing into work and obedient, passive citizenship (hopeful, perhaps, for the restoration to the status of subjects of a restored kaiser), many people in the thirties closed their eyes and merely hoped for the best.

My mother, on the other hand, was always interested in politics and in the entire spectrum of the arts, music, and literature. Although her disappointment with Russia's betrayal of the workers' movement caused her to give up her active involvement in it, she always remained strongly interested in what was going on in politics. She did not have any illusions about the direction in which Hitler would lead Germany—except for the most bizarre of his plans, like destroying the Jews.

SKETCHES BY FRITZ'S DAD, WILHELM JAENSCH, CREATED FREE HAND FROM MEMORY DURING THE TERRIBLE DAYS AT THE END OF WWII.

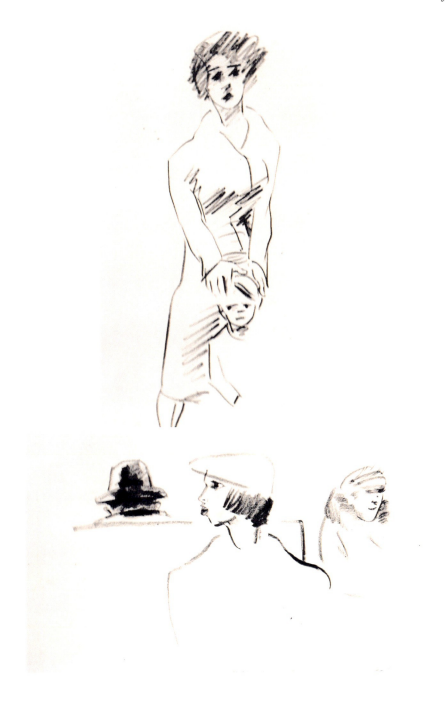

Steinstr. 17a.

Der Zwillingsteich.

Unsere Küche.

Blick aus dem fenster der Wohnstube.

Pregel am Holsteiner Damm.

Binnenhafen, von neuer Eisenbahnbrücke gesehen.

Steindamm, Blick vom Heumarkt zur Poststraße.

Schloßteich mit Burgkirche.

Morgenritt in Carolinenhof.

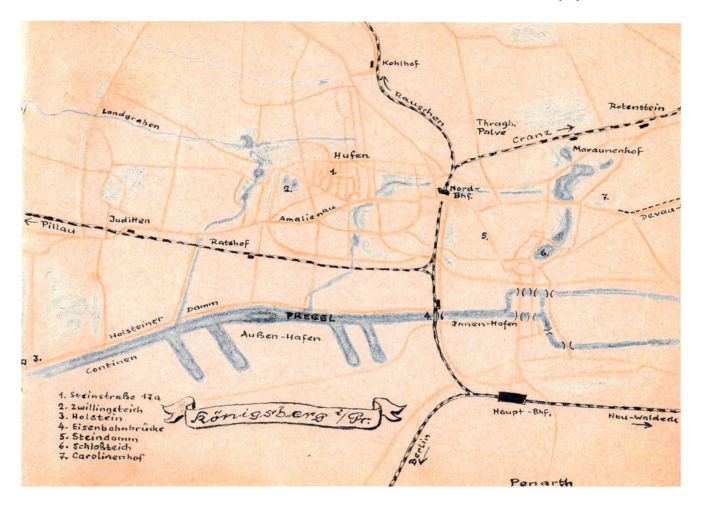

1. Steinstraße 17a
2. Zwillingsteich
3. Holstein
4. Eisenbahnbrücke
5. Steindamm
6. Schloßteich
7. Carolinenhof

Königsberg i/Pr.

My Ancestors on My Father's Side

My father, Wilhelm Jaensch, explains:

Picture 1: This picture shows my grandfather Jaensch. He was a teacher in a village school in Sensburg County in East Prussia's Masurian region. Next to him are his wife, Louise, née von Fritschen, and six of their twelve children. Only one of the children was a girl, Clara. You see her on the left side of the picture. On the outer right side, you see Arthur. He became my father later in life. About the other four boys, I have no information.

Picture 2: This picture shows my mother's father by the name of Feller. He was master tailor in the regiment of dragoons, stationed in Tilsit, East Prussia. His wife's birth name was Kretschmann. They had three children: Marie, Helene, and Wanda. Helene married my father, Arthur, in 1900. Father was a sergeant in an infantry regiment. He had signed up for twelve years of active duty. People called such a one a "twelve-ender." Father's obligatory service ended three years after his wedding. After he received his discharge papers, he started a middle-class career as a clerk in a court of law.

Picture 3: In this picture, you see my parents, each near the end of life. Before the outbreak of the war of 1914–1918, my father was clerk in a court of law. During that war and thereafter, he was a field officer in a troop-supply department. Hence the uniform. He died at age fifty-two in Königsberg. My mother died at seventy-seven when she was with us in Pech (near Bad Godesberg at the Rhine River).

Auf diesem Bild siehst Du meinen Großvater Jaensch, der in einem Dorf des Kreises Sensburg/Ostpreußen (Masuren) Lehrer gewesen ist. Zudem siehst Du auf dem Bild seine Ehefrau Louise geb, von Fritschen und sechs der zwölf Kinder aus dieser Ehe; nur eines der Kinder war ein Mädchen namens Clara. Du siehst sie am linken Rand des Bildes. Am rechten Rand siehst Du den Knaben Arthur, der später mein Vater wurde. Uber die vier anderen Knaben bin ich nicht informiert.

Auf diesem Bild siehst Du den Vater meiner Mutter, den Zuschneidermeister Feller des Dragonerregiments in Tilsit Ostpreußen. Er war verheiratet mit ein geb. Kretschmann. Ihre Kinder waren: Marie, Helene und Wanda. Die Helene heiratete 1900 meinen Vater, der damal noch Sergeant in einem Infanterieregiment war. Er hatte sich s.Zt. zu zwölf Jahren Militärdienst verpflichtet gehabt; im Volksmund hieß so einer "Zwölf ender." Diese Verpflichtung endete für meinen Vater drei Jahre nach seiner Hochzeit. Dann bekam er seinen Zivilversorgungsschein und begann seine mittlere Laufbahn bei einem Amtsgerich.

Auf diesem Bild siehst Du meine Eltern je in ihrer letzten Lebenszeit. Mein Vater war vor dem Krieg 1914–1918 Gerichtssekretär gewesen, dann im Krieg und nach ihm Intendantursekretär, also bei einer Truppen-Versorgungs behörde; daher auch die Uniform. Er starb 1919, 52 Jahre alt, in Königsberg.

Meine Mutter starb, 77 Jahre alt, 1953 bei uns in Pech.

I did not consciously get acquainted with Jewish people at all until 1952 when Hannah Arendt came to Frankfurt/Main. Unbeknownst to me, one of my childhood friends in Königsberg in 1938 and 1939, Helmut Kohn, must have been Jewish. After the war, Mother explained that names like Kohn, Kohen, or Kogon were of Jewish origin. Helmut was one of my closer friends, almost as close as Gerhard Bloess, whose father was at that time civilian guard of French prisoners of war. I remember admiring Helmut's parents. They both were slender and not too tall. They always walked arm in arm in lockstep, and

I liked the sound of their footsteps on the sidewalk. They did not wear the yellow star, and we kids did not much care what faith each of us belonged to.

The first time I saw that phenomenon of a yellow star worn on a man's overcoat was on my way to school in 1941, the year the United States was drawn into World War II.

A classmate noticed the yellow star on the man's business suit and said, "Spit at him."

I said, "Why?"

He said, "See that star? He can't do anything to you."

What happened there between us children was my introduction to Germany's shame and crime: the outrage my country committed against the Jewish people. To the credit of the grown-ups in my childhood, they did not burden my young mind with that hatred of Jewish people the German government demanded of all of us. However, they could not prevent the consequences of my ignorance. When my schoolmate told me to spit at the man who wore the yellow star, he caught me in a moral trap. Spitting at people was totally outside of my upbringing. That gentleman spoke our language. Except for that star, he wore the same kind of clothing every other man wore at that time. The street where we met him, the Koerterallee, was in the wealthy part of town—doctors' and lawyers' villas with wrought-iron fences and a riding path up the middle. To me, the gentleman looked no different than any other man we met on our way to school—and like my father or any of our neighbors whose children were my playmates on the big meadow behind my grandma's home. My elders expected me to wish the gentleman a good day—"guten Tag"—in passing. But the time of the good days was long over in Germany of 1941. The greeting enforced and demanded was the hailing of the dictator, Hitler.

All the Jewish people in Germany and in the countries Germany conquered during that war were forced by government decree to wear that yellow star. Millions of our Jewish fellow Europeans were first deprived of human dignity and literally burned up by order of our government during those years. This is what we remember today as the Holocaust. At that time, as a child, I did not understand that such killing was going on—or that that process began with spitting at people I had been brought up to treat with respect.

It was done by my government in mine and every other German's name. Therefore, as a German by birth, I accept and bear the burden of that responsibility and the mandate to see that it never happens again.

In normal times, I would not have had to walk to school along that beautiful, wealthy part of town where we boys met the man with the yellow star, but it was wartime. My neighborhood school, the

Krausschule, was transformed into a military hospital. My mother's absence and that longer way to school were the first two impacts of that war. The third, soon at hand, were bombs falling on the city.

Bombs, paraphrasing Margaret Boveri, are amazing unifiers of ideologically opposed populations.[*] While they fell, anyone who could sought shelter. Thereafter, at the all clear sound of the sirens, Nazi and anti-Nazi together went out to shovel the rubble.

I remember the first time I heard the sirens' howling alarm! All the tenants of Steinstrasse 17 gathered in the basement space that had been set aside as a bomb shelter. It was evening. We thought we heard remote explosions. In the morning, one of my playmates had something to show. He had been downtown and picked up a *Bombensplitter*, a metal fragment from a bomb. He handed it to me, and I felt strange holding the jagged fragment in hand—and well I might have. That strange fragment somehow violated my childhood's sense of safety and trust in the people who inhabited my world with me. The fragment, of course, also stirred my curiosity, especially inasmuch as the war, which it portended and symbolized, had not violated me and had not entered my conscience yet with any hint of alarm.

If the effect of bombs united opponents in the common necessity of rescue and rubble removal, there existed in the wake of that war a similar fate that threw opponents together as heirs of Holocaust and Hitler regime––heirs of those who acquiesced or supported the regime on one hand and opponents and victims on the other.

Germans all, we all are saddled with that heritage. How do we deal with that without feeling guilty? We must deal with it in order to discern the advent of similar events in the future. This is difficult because while forces like racism and violence exhibit recognizable symptoms, its advent is seldom the same in history. The way the malady runs its course and eventually exits the scene is never the same in appearance.

In contemplating these difficulties, it would be useful, first of all, to consider the principle involved in every flare-up of the malady, whether the flare-up is large or small. The amount of resentment leading to violence is not crucial, but the nature of it is in principle. Seldom does the devil approach like an SS battalion did Babi Yar in Kiev, where thousands of Jewish people were shot dead. The more common experience is the approach of evil with the tools of fascination, temptation, and instilling fear on a small scale. The igneous property of fire is the same, whether concentrated around the wick of a candle or raging in a forest fire. The igneous quality needs discerning.

---

[*] Margaret Boveri, *Tage des Ueberlebens* (Munich: DTV, 1970).

Jewish cemetery in Worms. The memorial stones in the middle are set over the remains of a thirteenth-century merchant and his beloved rabbi.

Der Zwillingsteich.

When I hear of or read about the horrendous crimes that were perpetrated in the time and country of my childhood, I still have difficulty understanding the extent of it in its entirety. However, the nature of it in principle is in retrospect plausible, mainly because of two experiences in the circle of my childhood perception. The character of these was prophetic.

Wherever people believe to be superior over fellow people, they try to portray the people they subdue as subhuman *(Untermenschen* in Hitlerite jargon). This is most often accomplished with deprivation. First, the targeted population is taken by stealth or overrun by force and imprisoned in ghettos, camps, or penitentiaries.

Then, often already on the way to confinement, the subdued people find themselves deprived of means to keep the body clean and clothed. In my childhood in Königsberg, I experienced both. One was the specter of a mob run amok and what appeared to me as a near rape. The other was the feeling of self-loathing because of my filthy body and clothing for lack of available sanitation.

The first episode I witnessed was in wintertime in Königsberg in a popular city park called Zwillingsteich, the park at the Twin Ponds. The Twin Ponds were connected with each other by three canals, each spanned by a footbridge. One winter day, I must have gone with the big boys from the neighborhood to the Twin Ponds. Once there, they went their own way and left me there. The frozen pond was full of people racing with skates over the ice or trying to skate in figures. All of a sudden, I saw a young lady little boys can only dream of. Dressed in winter leotards, the way you'd see them in Olympic winter competitions, she skated her figures perfectly. I could not take my eyes off her. All the other skaters made way for her or stopped to watch her.

However, some of the bigger guys started to make remarks as they moved in on her. Other men joined in taunting the beautiful girl until she had no more room on the ice to skate her figures. She skated away under one of the bridges, and she tried to continue her practice on the other pond. The brutes would not let her. She tried to get away from them, but they pursued her relentlessly, making remarks and howling with laughter. Nobody would step in to stop them. Finally, she skated to shore and landed right next to me. Tears ran down her face as she sat in the snow and started to take off her skates. When they saw they had her defeated and forced her off the ice, they roared off like a herd of monkeys tired of their play.

The beautiful girl—she must have been about fifteen years old—kept on crying as she finished taking off her skates. I wanted so much to console her, but I stood as if rooted to the spot, too shy to speak. At the same time, I was conscious of the fact that I also was a boy, a little edition, as it were, of the big types who had caused her tears.

This episode taught me something of big mobs running out of control––much as that segment of the German people did during the *Kristallnacht,* when mobs of German people, led on by units of Nazi storm troopers (SA) smashed the storefronts of Jewish-owned stores, dragged Jewish people into the streets, and humiliated, injured, and killed many of them. I did not witness that outrage, but that scene at the Twin Ponds helped me understand the essence of what had gone wrong.

Another childhood experience helped me understand a method that a regime in power, like the German Nazi regime, would use to mark people as "lesser humans." A captive and imprisoned people would be deprived of sanitation and hygiene. Something comparable happened to me, albeit not under any official duress.

The episode happened late in 1939, I think. Mother had already been taken away from us, but my dad was still working at the police station in Königsberg. For a while, my aunt Elisabeth, the wife of Mother's brother Helmut, came from Quedlinburg to help our grandmother care for my little sister and me. When Aunt Elisabeth had to return to her work in Quedlinburg and to her elderly mother, Father hired a young lady, Miss Loerke, to help Grandma care for us kids.

Miss Loerke grew very fond of my dad and tried to get his attention as much as she could. One day, she decided to visit Father at his work. She bundled my little sister into the baby stroller, and I held on to the handle and walked along. The police station where Dad worked was a three-story Victorian-style house with a garden around it and a wrought iron fence. Miss Loerke left the stroller in the garden and asked me to stay with it and to watch it while she took my little sister upstairs to visit Father in his office.

Quite some time went by, and I "had to go." There were people passing by on the street, but I was shy and didn't dare ask a stranger to help me. More time went by—lots of time—and I grew more and more desperate. I needed a toilet; otherwise, I would be in trouble. I looked around for some hidden corner or a bush I could get behind, but every place was in plain view of the street. I cried. It did not enter my mind that I could simply go into the house and ask someone where the toilet was. Children did what they were told, and there was nobody there to tell me anything. I jumped up and down, tried to sit down, twisted, and cried. I finally had to let things go their way.

Miss Loerke, as you might imagine, was thoroughly disgusted with me. She did not hit me, but she scolded incessantly. I did not even hear her words. I was so terrorized by that inescapable dilemma. If somebody had threatened to kill me, it would have been no worse. I did not get cleaned up until we got home, which was a good five city blocks away.

After that experience, I knew the kind of terror that was transformation from a normal child to a "subhuman," beneath the contempt of even myself. After that episode, Miss Loerke did not stay much longer with us.

The Struggle with Divorce and Regime-Imposed Living

Years later, my parents told me how they struggled through their marriage breakup and their subsequent separate decision-making.

Mother's brother Hans Erich asked Father to try to contact a cousin of his in Berlin. Rumor had it that he was someone of importance in the gestapo. Perhaps he could do something to shorten Mother's sentence. Meanwhile, my uncle suggested that Father should go through with the divorce and remarry Mother upon her release. The whole thing could, of course, backfire. The cousin, with whom Father had had no contact for years, could easily have felt offended and as a result sent Mother to death instead of liberty. In a dictatorial system, such as Hitler's Third Reich, much harm and death is dealt through arbitrary actions on the part of many officials in subordinate positions. So many grudges and vengeful passions are let loose, which multiply the destructive outcomes of the basic ideology and orders from the top. My father did not feel up to that hazardous course.

He decided instead to ask one of my mother's cousins, Hanna Riebensahm, to marry him. The members of the Riebensahm family were fond of giving each other nicknames. Mother's cousin Hanna suffered from severe osteoporosis. Her habitually drawn-up shoulders suggested to her siblings and cousins the aspect of a marabou stork. So they called her "Marabu." She was Aunt Marabu to me.

Aunt Marabu had a wonderful sense of humor and would, as the owner of a kindergarten in Königsberg, have been an ideal caretaker for my sister and me, but she considered herself too old for my father. She said, "Wilhelm, you are marrying a grandma. Why not marry Hedel instead of me?" Aunt Marabu spoke of her and my mother's cousin Hedwig Riebensahm, the second youngest of six siblings whose parents administered the government domain called Schaaken at the Kuren Lagoon of the Baltic Sea. Schaaken's manor house was a onetime castle of the German Knights of the Cross. East Prussia was dotted with castles of the German Knights in various stages of usage or ruin. Schaaken was one of the few in use until the Red Army's conquest in 1944.

While my father was agonizing over a possible surrogate mother for my sister and me, my mother was in Königsberg's jail for pretrial confinement and interrogation. The sense of responsibility a person in that predicament had was awesome. The slightest mention of any name, however inadvertent or casual, surely resulted in imprisonment and violence for unsuspecting friends and acquaintances from long ago—no matter where they were or what they ever did or did not do.

Mother came out of that trial with a fairly lenient sentence of three and a half years in Cottbus Prison. On the way there, while waiting with a group of prisoners at Königsberg's main railway station, Mother happened to be placed close to the edge of the platform. When the train pulled in, in her dejection, she earnestly contemplated throwing herself under the wheels. She thought, *The children, the children!* That thought kept her from letting go of life, and it energized her relentless efforts, despite the gestapo threats, to regain custody of us after her release from prison.

Mother, Hedel, Fritz, Johanna, and Klaus

Hedwig Riebensahm had agreed to take in my sister and me at Schleuduhnen. Schleuduhnen, a farm, was four hundred *morgen* (about eight hundred acres), and it belonged to her sister Felicitas (Aunt Fee) and her husband, Horst Doepner. Hedel was caring for her sister's four sons: Axel, Klaus, Felix, and Hans. My sister and I moved to Schleuduhnen and into Mother Hedel's care just in time. It coincided with our father's call-up to active military duty. Now both of our parents were gone.

The grown-ups who surrounded me were National Socialist true believers. Uncle Horst, a county supervisor and farm owner, was quite highly placed in the party and was exempt from service at the front. Not that being in the party was necessarily anything special. Upon Hitler's assumption of power in 1933, he used the incident of the burning of the Reichstag, the parliament building in Berlin, to invoke an emergency empowerment act, provided for in the Constitution. After a majority in the Reichstag voted in favor of granting him the exceptional powers, he then made use of them to eliminate all political parties other than his National Socialist Party. The act was known as the *Gleichschaltung*, the unification of all social institutions under the authority of the Nazi Party. No organization was henceforth allowed to exist that was not NS-something. That included the county of Bartenstein, where my uncle was supervisor. It, incidentally, also included the youth choir of Königsberg's radio station where I was a choirboy after Aunt Hedel and Father married and returned for a while to live in Königsberg.

Father and Aunt Hedel did get married in Schleuduhnen. Aunt Hedel became "Little Mother Hedi." We called her *Hedimuttchen*, and we loved her dearly. In later years, her cousin Hella, our mother, also came to call her by that well-beloved name—and so did my four Doepner cousins. Love under the wings of her protection conquered all ideologies.

I remember that wedding day on my uncle's farm because it featured for us children that absolute rarity in those days of war: ice cream!

Aunt Marabu chuckled with mockery when she recalled the ceremony because it was modeled exactly on the Lutheran wedding ceremony. Uncle Horst officiated, walking up to the "altar" to the strains of a Schubert Impromptu in the great hall of the manor house. And just as in church, the congregation arose as Uncle Horst lifted Hitler's *Mein Kampf*—and not the Bible—faced us, and read from it.

The marriage held until death parted the couple long after the end of the Nazi nightmare. For me, Hitler's usurpation of the church's ritual (as well as Stalin's) was no simple matter. The fact that these dictators copied the Christian ritual testified to its intrinsic solemn power. The revelation of its falsification could be painful and confusing for a child searching for what was true and reliable, but I was spared that pain for the time being, not knowing church yet.

Hedel and Wilhelm Jaensch

Let me reemphasize a point I have made a few paragraphs back. In a totalitarian regime, such as Hitler's Third Reich in Germany, the evil in principle resides in the person at the top, in Hitler, the author of the ideology of strident racism and violent conquest. Nevertheless, the implementation of that policy depends at every stage upon the character of those who are compelled to follow the general order. The annals of that time abound with reports both of arbitrary savagery licensed from the top and the quiet deeds of courage and imagination that often assuaged the worst and helped people survive.

In my experience, the latter might have come about by dint of the adults thinking that I was too young to understand anything. Nevertheless, I do credit the grown-ups of my childhood with refraining from aggressively indoctrinating me with Nazi ideology. The years I lived as a privileged member of the manor house on my uncle's farm, Schleuduhnen, had every ingredient for making of me an enthusiastic adherent of the swastika flag and all it stood for. Instead, I learned to love the country, the animals, and the working people on the farm, especially the Russian people, prisoners of war, who worked there. And in spite of the Nazi milieu in which I found myself, the cross of Christ proved a superior beacon for me than the hooked cross of Hitler. I cannot say why or plead any special virtue. As a compromised child of a "fallen" woman in the eyes of official ideologues, I ought to have been subject to special emphasis on loyalty to the führer. Instead, I experienced the love of my extended family most of all.

Schleuduhnen made me forget the perils of war and the sorrows of my parents' absence. I roamed the fields and the barns on the farm with my cousin Axel. The cows and the pigs were not nearly as interesting to us as the horses and those who worked with them. Among those who handled the four-in-hand teams of workhorses were our Russian friends, Philip, Timofey, Petri the cook, and a few others, with whom Axel and I got closely acquainted.

Uncle Horst, vaguely adhering to his duty, I suppose, tried to dissuade us from fraternizing with "those people." However, in time, he gave up trying to enforce the segregation law of the Reich and let his oldest son and I enjoy our companionship with the "enemy." They would lift us onto the side horse to ride out into the fields for plowing in spring, the hay harvest in June, and the grain harvest in August. On the way out, out of earshot of the farm, the men sang the songs of their homeland. I have heard them several times since, over Red Army loudspeakers after the war, and much later in Moscow's Kremlin. My special love for the Russian people, I believe, dates back to my childhood acquaintance with those Russians on my uncle's farm.

After my father and Hedel were married, we returned for a time to live in my grandmother's apartment in Königsberg, although we visited Schleuduhnen frequently. That happened to be the time when my mother was released from prison. Defying official orders to stay away from us, she came to my school one day and called to me during lunch break. She later told me it was the saddest reunion she could have imagined.

That first meeting at the school yard after three and a half years of absence did not go well. I acted strangely noncommittal and monosyllabic, my mother later recalled, almost embarrassed. When she asked me how things were at home, I looked away and said something about "all new furniture."

Subsequent visits, which both my father and my stepmother permitted, went much better. Mother took us to the town of Neuhaeuser by the Baltic Sea or to the nearby forest of Metgethen to look for mushrooms and berries. I remember Mother teaching us music: Mozart canons, the Quempas Christmas songs, and songs from her days in the youth movements. In this way, my sister's and my relationship with Mother was reestablished and grew strong. However, Mother very seldom came to be with us.

Mother's intense efforts to regain custody of her children were waylaid by one of her cousins, a lawyer from the extreme right wing of the family. He felt that my mother Hella's reappearance from her imprisonment was a nuisance. He ordered Mother into his office, and he told her that she better disappear from being near her children—unless she wanted him to make her disappear for good. Facing that unexpected death threat from a relative of hers made Mother relent and seek work in Berlin.

Mother was caught unaware in extremely hostile surroundings. Her situation was not unlike St. Peter being caught in the high priest's courtyard, close to his imperiled friend, and faced with a life-threatening vulnerability, his Galilean accent. Likewise, my mother, staying close to her children, found her life threatened by one who knew her vulnerability. She was ordered to "never see them again." Who in his compassionate right mind would want to accuse such a person of cowardliness for backing off into the night of bitter tears?

Mother was a person with uncommon courage, but she never made any fuss about it. She quietly did what her conscience prompted her to do. In 1937, for example, when Hitler's regime was firmly entrenched in Germany, Hannah Arendt had already fled Germany. Hannah's mother, Mrs. Beerwald, still lived in Königsberg, not far from where we lived, in the Busolt Strasse. Mother visited Mrs. Beerwald regularly, which made Father quite nervous. However, he did not forbid Mother to go. Mrs. Beerwald told Hella, her daughter's trusty friend, to mind the danger to which she exposed herself when she visited a Jewish woman. She suggested it might be better to end her visits. In later years, whenever the subject came up, Mother Hella said, "But she was like a mother to me. How could I have acted as if I didn't know her?"

The voice of reason could have instructed her: "Ignorance made you so brave, while others tried to warn you." An angel guarded her ignorance that time.

Hannah, now in Paris, succeeded in getting her mother out of Königsberg just in a nick of time. That must have been early in 1939.

In Berlin, late in 1942—after Mother's release from gestapo prison—she was ordered to work caring for the two children of a Nazi functionary. She was closely watched and unreasonably suspected of underground activity. Once she turned on a light switch by mistake. She promptly turned it off again, but that was imputed unto her as "signaling the enemy."

In that very time and place, it so happened that one day to Mother's great surprise (joyful in any circumstance but this one) a Jewish couple, Mr. and Mrs. Stern* entered the elevator cab Mother was riding up to the apartment. The Sterns were very close friends from Mother's youth in Königsberg. To Mother, they were Aunt and Uncle Stern.

Uncle Wilhelm Stern was so surprised and happy to see "Little Hella" that he wanted to greet her with a hug.

His wife noticed how frightened my mother was. With a warning glance, she prevented him from giving her that hug. The elevator was not the closed type people ride up and down in high-rise buildings. The elevators in Berlin went up the center of the stairwell and were completely open to view. In 1942, in Berlin, to be Jewish or to be a friend of Jews was a death sentence. I don't know if Mother cried bitter tears over that forced denial of her friends (as Peter was reputed to have shed). What I do know is that Mother mustered the courage to stay in touch with the Sterns.

Shortly after that surprise encounter, Mother learned that Uncle Stern had fallen seriously ill and was in need of hospital care. She went to visit Pastor Poelchau on Uncle Stern's behalf to see if the pastor could recommend a hospital where a Jewish patient could be halfway safe. Reverend Poelchau was chaplain at Tegel Prison, which was where Dietrich Bonhoeffer was imprisoned. He was known "on the grapevine" to be trustworthy. Reverend Poelchau recommended a Catholic hospital he knew of, but before Mother could get the message to the Sterns, she learned that Uncle Wilhelm Stern had taken his own life. There were many such quietly courageous men and women and their stories. Mother's was one of these.

Courageous pronouncements of readiness are often enough made in ignorance, the same ignorance that, ex post facto, pronounces judgment. But when the cock crows, the mortal danger you are in stares you in the face. How you act at that moment counts. Thanks be to God for all whose courage does not fail them.

Back in Königsberg, Father and Stepmother Hedel, when they learned of the lawyer cousin's threats against Mother Hella's life, decided to grant Mother time to visit with us. That decision was not free

---

* Mr. and Mrs. Stern. It occurs to me that the Sterns were, perhaps, the parents of Hannah's first husband, Günter Stern, who later changed his name to Günter Anders.

of danger either. It went against official orders. Mother, while grateful, never relinquished her quiet insistence to have her children.

Suddenly, out of the blue, as it were, Mother's life was imperiled once again. This time, it was not by Nazi directives or the ever-increasing bombing raids; it was by me. Prisoners, once released, were under threat of death forbidden to reveal any of their experiences, especially to children.

The incidents that imperiled my mother's freedom can serve to illustrate the hazards of everyday communication for people in a totalitarian state. Mother always stayed with friends when she came on furlough from Berlin. Someone trusted, like, for instance, Aunt Marabu, would fetch Johanna and me and bring us to her. One such home of friends I liked was the apartment of the Luttercort sisters at the back of the zoo. I liked it because I could look into the zoo and see the American bison. It could well have been there that I overheard my mother in conversation with her friends mentioning a man they knew who died in prison. During one of the earlier visits with Mother, during an outing to the sea coast, I had asked why she had been away so long.

She said, "I did not love the führer enough." That was a political statement.

I promised Mother not to repeat it at home.

Apparently, I said, "You will see if I am a blabbermouth or a master of silence."

That promise I kept, mainly, I believe, because as soon as I came to my father and stepmother's home, I totally forgot my conversations with Mother.

Hella Jaensch

The story of the man who died in prison was different. I did not feel that it had anything to do with Mother or the führer.

One day, the grown-ups in Father and Mother Hedel's home talked about a man who died, and I said, "Oh, I heard about a man who died in prison!"

My stepmother had spoken of her only brother who had died in the war, and she thought that her cousin Hella, my mother, had told me he had died in prison.

I can imagine that an American, reading this little vignette today, is bored to tears, yet it was a miracle that it did not lead to Mother's arrest and death. It is so difficult to convey the perils of life in an earlier time to a new generation.

4

———◆———

CHAPTER

Der Volksempfänger

It could, perhaps, be understood that the carefree life on my uncle's farm did not provide a connection in my child's mind between that and the promises Hitler held out to young people like me. But there was an instrument that was calculated to have an irresistible pull on the minds of the German people. That instrument was the radio. (There was as yet no television).

My grandma had one of those little black boxes, called *Volksempfänger* (the people's receiver), that inexpensive terminal for the regime's propaganda. Every home had one, and it was every German's civic duty to listen to every one of Hitler's speeches and to most speeches of his propaganda minister, Joseph Goebbels. The speeches went pretty much over my head, but it was quite different with the music.

Grandma and Aunt Skaga, a friend of hers who came to visit daily, would sit in the kitchen while a singer crooned over the little Volksempfänger some song about a "brave little soldier's wife," or "Lillie Marlene," a hit that crossed all fighting frontiers. All of a sudden, a different tune broke into the program: "The Symphonic Poem Number 3, Le Prélude" by Franz Liszt! After a few phrases of the rousing fortissimo part of that piece, a voice broke in and said, "Deutsche Panzerverbände auf dem Vormarsch im Osten" (German tank columns advancing in the east). Then, with Liszt continuing in the background, the announcer gave the details of the battles. There was no mistaking the fact that here was mention of German glory and conquest … the obliteration of "the shame of Versailles," the reestablishment of the proper glory of the Germanic ancestors, Emperor Barbarossa's resurrection, and the triumph of the führer's will. And I knew—because I had asked the grown-ups in Schleuduhnen—that my father, as a soldier, was a part of all that Liszt-inspired greatness.

Goebbels's propaganda machine was extremely effective in keeping the German population focused on the war effort long past the point of exhaustion and of the creeping doubt about the just cause of the war and the leader's ability to force the victory.

Germany conducted the Second World War like a giant predator, and it sucked the economic and human energy lifeblood out of all the conquered countries. But after 1942, when the German advance was stopped and went into reverse, the energy to continue the war was soon nearly depleted. Goebbels's propaganda was hard-pressed to invent new reasons for the population to stay in the fight. At that point, fear of "the savage Bolshevik" and the "pollution of the pure race" by the raping enemy was increasingly used. Toward the end of 1944, Germany's will to war was but a hollow tree. With all the pirated energy consumed, it remained standing there until the bitter end. The thing that kept it standing and the war going was in the end the effectiveness of propaganda and "the Volksempfänger."

The tools of propaganda are, of course, not restricted to totalitarian regimes. Propaganda is a refunctioning* of historical events to suit the present ideological agenda of a people's government. The Vietnam War might serve as an example from the United States. In the 1970s, the majority of the American population grew tired of the casualties and the demoralizing effect of the war and wanted only "to get out of that place." Barely ten years later, under a new administration, that same war was declared a victory for the soldiers in the field—and treason on the part of the protesting civilian population. It was a successful propaganda feat, benign, perhaps, by comparison with what happened in Germany's Third Reich. Nevertheless, Germans know it well. The First World War was rationalized into a victory for them in the same manner.

In Germany, in 1944, the time of reckoning had come. The summer on the farm was beautiful. We children had so much fun that we almost overlooked the grown-ups' worried faces and conversations.

Father came to Schleuduhnen on furlough and left again. He and my uncle were looking at a map one day.

I sidled up to them, looked at Father, and asked, "Where are you fighting?" I pointed close to the Lithuanian border.

---

* German *umfunktionieren*, a term coined by Bertolt Brecht.

Father said, "We stand much farther east—around Vilna!" Vilna was very close!

One day, Axel and I saw a new sight on the highway: an unfamiliar horse-drawn wagon, piled high with luggage and furniture, a cow in tow. By and by, there were more such wagons, and a few of them turned in at my uncle's farm. They were refugees from the front. We welcomed them and gave shelter to them and their horses. The trickle of refugees soon became a steady stream driving westward—away from the approaching Red Army.

Hitler's order was that everybody stays. It was a vain attempt to make the army fight harder to stay the onslaught, which thereafter was changed into an attempt to keep the refugees from clogging the paths of retreat for the army.

One night in August 1944, we all went outside and looked toward Königsberg. The city was under heavy bombardment and engulfed in fire. My mother later told me that the bells of the domed church rang in the upsurge of the fire until the city died in the flames. My uncle went to the city and, coming back, reported chaos and much loss of life.

Nevertheless, life on the farm regained its own harvest rhythm. We brought in the rye, the oats, and the barley, and late in September and early in October, we brought in the potatoes and beets.

November was approaching. The refugees left us, and our leaving also was at hand. My uncle decided to send my stepmother westward by train and to have her take my two youngest cousins, Felix and Hans, and my sister and me. His wife and their two oldest sons, Axel and Klaus, stayed to leave in the dead of winter with the horse-drawn wagon.

The day of departure was a cold November day. The train was slow in coming. The signals no longer worked properly. A munitions train was going east, and then ours came. The destination was a little village, Jahnsbach, in Annaberg County in the Erzgebirge (Ore Mountains), close to the Czech border. It was there that the Holocaust caught up with me before the war ended. I have related that experience to my grandchildren in a letter as follows:

Jahnsbach

I never will forget the day I stood there, stunned. From horizon to horizon, the sky above this town was filled with American liberator bombers, their bellies full of bombs. The ground trembled with their roaring. They were headed for Dresden.

5

CHAPTER

Lest We Forget!

Alameda
October 13, 1993

My dear grandchildren:

Irecently witnessed a *60 Minutes* segment about Channel 1, the school channel. The reporter was told that the commercials of that channel were designed to lure kids into buying stuff they don't need. That ought not to be surprising to anybody; what else are commercials for?

But then there was the allegation that the channel broadcasts propaganda for foreign governments. As an example, they showed a commercial that advertised the German town of Dachau as "actually a quaint, nice, clean German town." It did mention, in passing, that there was a concentration camp near that town during Hitler's rule. But the commercial quickly relegated that to the past, no longer worth mentioning. But if we don't remember, we can never learn. We'll simply run on DNA—instinct, like a cow in the pasture—instead of thinking about what happened; and if it was bad, thinking about how we can choose a better way.

I lived—as I have told you earlier—as a little refugee kid with my stepmother, Hedi, my little sister, Johanna, and my cousins Felix and Hans in Jahnsbach in the Ore Mountains. The next town down the highway past the school and the grocer and the town hall was called Thum. There, my mom, Hella, your Omi, lived and worked during the last days of the war. The year was 1945. In April of that year, my little sister Angelika was born. I remember that day. Hedi Muttchen took me along in the morning. With a hand-drawn cart, we went to the coal merchant and got a sack of coal to cook with. Hedi Muttchen and I pushed and pulled that cart of coal up the steep, long grade through the whole village to the Lindner home, where we were quartered. That evening, Hedi Muttchen walked a good mile to the home of the midwife lady, and that night, Angelika was born. Just in time. Because when Muttchen returned home with her a few days later, the war was starting to come ever closer to us. The Russian army approached from the other side of Thum, and the Americans approached from our side of the village.

The highway that entered our village from the side where the Americans came from wound up and over the top of a saddle in the mountains. I banded together with a bunch of refugee kids since the local kids didn't like us too much. We were intruders—strangers—although we too spoke their language, only a different dialect. One day, this kid and I went up toward that little forest on the rim of the mountain, where the highway descended to the neighboring village. We had heard some shots fired there, and we were curious. There in the woods along the highway was a veritable arsenal of weapons of every description and cars that had run out of gas. A bunch of kids from the neighboring villages were there, helping themselves to the guns and pistols and firing those weapons into the trees—until a couple of German soldiers with white armbands came down the road and told us sharply to get out of there. "This is a tragedy," said one of the men. "This place is within the range of the American guns. If they hear you, we and you are finished, understand?"

These soldiers, wearing white armbands, who had thrown away their weapons in the woods, were among the signs that the war was really coming to an end. The only thing we really feared was the question how the victors would treat us.

We had reason to be apprehensive. You remember me telling you of that incident a number of years earlier during my first year of school? A fellow pupil on the way to school told me to spit on a Jewish man who wore the yellow star. I refused, but the German people as a whole did not. Instead, Jewish people were rounded up year after year, herded into concentration camps, brutalized, and killed. Now, in May 1945, we Germans—young and old—had reason to fear the victors' vengeance.

Among the strange processions of the broken-down familiar order, there was one that topped all the images of misery I had known until then. I was in the center of the village of Jahnsbach, on the main street across from the grocery store. I don't remember what brought me to that spot, but there I was. A troop of German soldiers armed with burp guns herded a troop of people up the street and onto that open place behind that grocery store. These people all wore striped pants and jackets and heavy wooden clogs on their feet. They were obviously exhausted and barely able to move, but the soldiers barked at them and urged them on. I shall never forget the last three of those men in striped clothes. Two held up a third man, whom they verily dragged along. His feet were no longer able to walk. He moaned and made gurgling sounds of pain.

I was absolutely wide-eyed and strangely embarrassed for that man. Only once in my life before that moment had I seen a man unable to walk. It was in Friedland by the Alle River Bridge, across from my uncle's house, where I saw that man stumble along and fall against the garden wall that went parallel to the road in that spot. "He's drunk," said my cousin Binchen.

This was the second time I saw a person incapable of walking. There, in Jahnsbach, there was an eerie, palpably uncomfortable silence among the grown-up onlookers who surrounded me. The soldiers' commands and the cries and moans of the prisoners overpowered their mumbled comments. At that moment, quite involuntarily, my voice issued forward loud and clear: "He's drunk!" And as if it was the answer to the vain search for an excuse, some of the grown-ups, fearing for their own hide, repeated that ignorant phrase. I have never forgotten. What happened there was what had gone wrong with Germany and with us Germans: ignorance and feigned ignorance and cowardly fear in the face of brute force. And more such convoys—prisoners on trucks and prisoners shuffling along, herded by gun-toting soldiers— came down the highway and through the village. The soldiers asked us civilians for some cigarettes (rare commodities then). I remember running home to ask Muttchen for some cigarettes for the soldiers—with no thought for what the prisoners might want.

Once that bizarre nightmare ended, we learned what those prisoners had wanted: a piece of bread, a draft of water, first of all. We too learned to beg for that; for now, the time had come for starvation. Lest we forget … lest we forget!

Grandpa Fritz

6

CHAPTER

The War

On that day, the wrong we had done to humanity in Germany burned itself indelibly into my mind. And with that realization, a question arose in my mind: What was my part in that wrongdoing? What should I have done differently? And how about my parents and their generation? These questions were not easy to answer then and there, and they have not gotten any easier to answer as time progressed.

Politics, the law of the land, and citizens' obligations under the law were all ineffective. Hitler had turned right and wrong upside down for the German people. After Germany's defeat, it became clearer to me that obeying the law of the land, doing the duty of a citizen (*Volksgenosse*, "people's comrade" in Third Reich parlance), honoring the flag, and fighting for your country were all bad. Disobeying and circumventing the law and the authorities of the state were the right things to do.

I was very fortunate that I was but ten years old when freedom from Hitler was achieved. Had I been older, I would have been a full-fledged member of the Hitler Youth organization. Toward the end of the war, fourteen-year-olds were being sent to the front. Joining the Hitler Youth was not a choice; it was *Dienst* (duty).

The German government obliged every boy and girl aged ten and above to attend daily Hitler Youth meetings after school. My official call-up came in Jahnsbach about a month before the end of the war. As a member of the *Rundfunkspielschaar,* the boys' choir at the radio station in Königsberg, I had by that time already been a quasi member of the Hitler Youth.

In Jahnsbach, I received notice to stay after school for *H. J. Dienst* (Hitler youth duty). I had no problem with that, and I remember I found it odd that many of my classmates tried to stay out of it in view of things to come. As a choirboy in Königsberg, I was never formally initiated. In Jahnsbach, in April 1945, I underwent the initiation ceremony with my class. We were led into a room in my school that was set apart just for that purpose. The room was filled with all kinds of flags and banners—all with the black swastika in a circular white field in the middle of a red cloth. Among all the flags, the most important was the *Blutfahne,* the blood-flag that represented a long line of flags that had all touched each other in special ceremonies. The first in line of these special flags was the one held by a *Sturmabteilungsmann,* a storm trooper or Nazi party street fighter, during Hitler's attempt to overthrow the Bavarian government in Munich in the 1920s. The coup was foiled in a confrontation with government military units. Some storm troopers were shot. Their blood was on the "blood flag," which Hitler elevated to the status of a religious national icon.

Facing that flag in that room full of flags, we were all admonished to be good Germans and to fight for the führer to the end. Thereafter, we went outside, and in the schoolyard, we practiced marching. I was good at marching, and I enjoyed immensely how marching is done and how to react to the commands the youth leader barked out at me. Like my father and my grandfathers, I had the makings of a good soldier.

Jahnsbach Church on Main Street

I am sure that as far as my classmates were concerned, I—this crazy refugee kid from the eastern provinces—was no doubt a real Nazi. However, at that time and in that place, I failed to make the connection in my mind between the persecution and torture imposed upon those human beings in striped clothing who were herded through our village and the ideology of "the Blutfahne." I just liked to sing, and I enjoyed marching.

On the other hand, I had seen enough Allied bombers filling the sky from horizon to horizon, fighter planes swooping low across the mountains and attacking our little narrow-gauge train, the sound of artillery in the distance, soldiers with white armbands, and convoys of utter misery to know that something was about to come to a terrible end.

During the last days of the war, I also heard a call I had faintly heard before. This was not a call to duty enforced by the state; it was a simple beckoning to come, listen, and look. As a refugee family with four little children and one on the way, my stepmother was entitled to receive one or two liters of milk every day. The farmer from whom we received the milk lived down the long street on the other side of the village. It was my duty to walk down there—past the church, the school, and the store—to fetch the milk. On Sundays, the bells in the twin-steepled church rang out. The door of the church stood ajar. I could hear the organ playing and the congregation singing. "Come, listen and look," said the inner voice.

One Sunday, I hid my little milk can in the shrubs, went up the steps, and peeked through the leaning door into the church. I didn't go in. Aware of time passing and my duty, I turned around, got my milk can, and went after the milk.

Duty, responsibility, and the curiosity about the calls to soul and mind: I barely realized the conflict of these various appeals to my sense of loyalty. Little did I know then that the call that issued through the church bells, the organ, and the singing congregation was the strongest of all.

7

What Happened, Mother?

It was May 1945. The Americans and Russians had met in the neighboring town of Thum, and the Russians had set up their command post there. The war was over. The new authorities first ordered us to hang white sheets out of the windows, but soon we were ordered to fly red flags because we were in the Russian occupation zone. All the red flags had a red circle where the swastikas had been removed.

One day, I was in the town hall with my grandmother. I pointed to the red flag bulging in the breeze and said, "A flag looks nice, whatever the color."

Grandma said, "Oh, it's just a rag on the wall."

Her comment put flags and their importance into perspective for me. Later, in school, we learned about William Tell and how he refused to salute a hat on a stick. Rag on a wall and hat on a stick? Imagine my astonishment eleven years hence when, as an immigrant to the United States, I was invited to a high school graduation where all the people, young and old, put their hands over their hearts and prayed fervently to "a rag on the wall." That experience whirled my perspective around once again.

Hedel and Hella: cousins, friends, and my mothers

My mother stayed close to us during the last few weeks of the war. She was able to leave Berlin and come to the Ore Mountains to work in the bookstore in the neighboring town of Thum. She also helped out in the household of the owner of one of the garment factories in town where silk stockings were manufactured. Her employer paid her with silk stockings, which were a precious commodity for us because Mother could barter them for food.

At war's end, my two mothers, Hedel, my father's wife, and Hella, my sister Johanna's and my mother, conferred and came to an agreement. My sister and I would go live in Thum with our mother. The two women also agreed to destroy the divorce documents, the wording of which would have been damaging to Father. I never learned what that wording was except that the document listed Mother as "the guilty party" in the divorce. Much more important for me was what my father told me the next time I saw him. He said, "The divorce and its circumstances notwithstanding, you and your sister were wanted and conceived in love." I can recommend that, where it is true, divorced parents do tell their children that fact about their genesis!

After my sister and I were safely transferred to our mother, my stepmother left Jahnsbach on a perilous trip to the town of Gentin on the Elbe River to bring her nephews Hans and Felix to their mother, my aunt Fe. Aunt Fe had made it to that town after a harrowing winter trek through Pommern. The Red Army had overtaken them with all the attendant suffering and hardships. I could not even guess the nature of those hardships. I know that Axel, my cousin and companion on his father's farm, had seen too much. When we met again a year hence, his nerves were severely afflicted. He burst into tears at the slightest provocation. By that time, they all had found a place to live on a farm, Kasmark, in Schleswig Holstein in the British occupation zone.

My sister and I lived with Mother in Thum. We were among many refugees quartered in the town's school building. Our most immediate problems were the lack of food and the vermin that made us break out with sores. In the best of times, the region of the Ore Mountains was poor. With the extra burden of the refugees, the situation was desperate. I went daily with a shopping bag from farm to farm, asking if they could spare one or two potatoes. In one embarrassing moment, a classmate of mine, a farmer's son, said, "No, we feed them to the chickens." I thought the farmers were mean, but they did have to protect their seed stock, which was verily under siege—if not outright attack. Quite a few people didn't bother begging; they simply helped themselves to the field crops, and some got caught.

One day I saw the strangest specter in the public square. Two women walked slowly along the street, side by side. Each had a bell and rang it. Over their shoulders, in front and back, they wore cardboard signs that stated: "I am a traitor to the people! I have stolen potatoes in the fields!" They were escorted by a policeman walking his bike.

Hella and Fritz Jaensch, mother and son

I was with a bunch of curious kids who followed the moving pillory scene, making comments all along. When Mother came home from work at the bookstore, I told her about it.

She scolded me severely and said, "Those women have a family to feed just like ours; they do what they can to get some food. Don't you dare ridicule them!" Then she told me about food procurement whenever bare survival is at stake—like, for instance, in prison. In such extreme situations, the normal laws of civic behavior bend, and the rule becomes much more: help yourself and then help your child or a friend. (From today's perspective, the rule might be compared to donning the oxygen mask in an airplane: first myself, then the child). In the extremes of war and starvation, women with children are always handicapped. They do many unsung deeds of heroism on behalf of their children.

"What are those women going to do now?"

Mother replied, "They are going to get food the best way they can."

Going into summertime made gathering food a little easier than it would have been in winter. There were nettles in the hedgerows and dandelions and sour grass in the meadows. Many gleaners were on the highways to glean what ears of grain they could find or gather the potatoes or beets that fell off the harvest wagons. Many traded linens, family heirlooms, or jewelry for food.

Mother was fortunate to have those silk stockings during the last weeks of the war. With those stockings in the knapsack, Mother, my sister, and I traveled to some of the smaller villages where there were not as many refugees as in Thum. She always went to the minister in town to learn where a farmer might be able to spare some potatoes.

One day, we traveled to the town of Großrückerswalde. The town had a beautiful old walled church, which had doubled as a defensive structure in the Middle Ages. The pastor there, Walter Schumann, took a special interest in our plight and sent us to farmers who could help us. Carrying the purchased potatoes back was always an arduous task. Trekking down the Skopau River Valley and up the steep slope on the other side, through several villages, seemed endless to me.

Whenever we were at Pastor Schumann's home, we shared in that family's food and their joyful expression of their faith. One day, I asked Mother if I could not become a Christian too.

Once she granted my request, Walter Schumann baptized my sister and me. He also became my godfather. My godmother was Edith Petrusky, the chaplain in Cotbus, where my mother had been imprisoned. At that time, being a godparent was a grave responsibility. Although the war was over, the situation was very unsettled—and godparents could be called upon to take in the children.

Pretty soon, it became clear that the Americans would not come to rule over us as we had hoped. Instead, the Red Army set up the military occupation government. Thum was apparently too small to have any sizable garrison of Russian soldiers, but the regional commander of the Red Army announced his desire to speak to the people of Thum.

We were ordered into the main square to listen as the new commander announced the law of the new order. A band on the raised platform played old Communist marching songs, including "The International," and other tunes that were new to me. I observed an older woman crying and fervently singing along. We stood in rows, filling the square for one hour, two hours, longer—but the commander never showed up. That was the first of many such mass meetings I attended, all with the same waiting pattern. It was, perhaps, arranged that way on purpose. As soon as something did seem to happen on the stage, the bored and restive people started cheering—and that cheering was what the photographers documented for the newspapers.

There was no television in those days—I saw my first TV in 1956 in America—but there was radio! The new regime made use of "the folk receiver" as efficiently as the previous order had. We learned over the airwaves what had happened in the concentration camps. People who lived close to the liberated camps were led there to see for themselves the mountains of corpses we had produced there under Hitler's orders. Those of us who lived farther away got an earful of propaganda instead. That kind of truth telling by means of the radio amounted to horror as pornography: the sound of whips almost always cracking down on female flesh, women screaming and moaning in pain. Having no visual effects to confirm the source of the sounds, the imagination was left to make up its own picture. I cannot now recall my reaction to the sounds from the radio, except to say that they were less immediate a conveyor of truth than was my witnessing of the men in striped suits being driven by German soldiers through the town of Jahnsbach. That was genuine, and it haunted me for many years.

The bookstore where my mother worked also had stacks of pamphlets for sale—all graphically describing people's horrendous experiences in the concentration camps. When I was visiting Mother at the bookstore, a customer picked up one of the yellow-bound brochures.

I said eagerly, "Descriptions from the concentration camps—all true!"

He looked at my mother with a faint smile.

Mother smiled too.

"Good salesman, your boy," the man said as he left.

Through thirteen years of Hitler's rule and Goebbels's propaganda, people had learned that "paper is patient." You can print anything on it. Sound waves work the same way. If you repeat the message long enough, people will repeat mindlessly whatever is said or printed. And as the weeks of Russian occupation grew into months and years, we learned that we had no reason to revise that basic insight.

Mother did not add horror to horror. She told me instead what it was that saw her through all the difficulties, both in prison and afterward during the bombing raids on Berlin. Safety, she explained, was in trustworthy friendship and in the development of a special intuition. In a prison situation, the variety of human character traits is, perhaps, more starkly evident than elsewhere.

Hella Jaensch

The individual guards each had their own way of enforcing the general order. Mother told me of an instance where a fellow prisoner returned to the cell from working in the kitchen. If you were detailed to the kitchen, it was understood that you would take care of your friends with some extra food—if you could. The woman was stopped by one of the guards and asked something that required that she take her arms from where she had crossed them in front of her. The two loaves of bread she was hiding fell out, which was enough of an infraction to send the woman to Ravensbrück concentration camp. The guard decided not to have seen anything, and the women in Mother's cell had extra bread that day instead of losing a companion.

The bonds of friendship and acts of human decency were the lifeline that upheld the hope of the people. It was a network of survival that helped the prisoner survive beyond the collapse of the Nazi regime. Mother taught us a song, which, she said, every prisoner knew—a victims' hymn of hope: "*Die Moorsoldaten*" ("The Swamp Soldiers"). Lamenting the conditions of imprisonment, the song confirms in its last lines the certain hope: "Not forever will we sorrow / Winter will not always be / One day we shall yet be saying / Homeland, homeland, we are free!"

After searching, Mother found friends of hers in Halle, a city with much less poverty than the villages of the Ore Mountains. We were able to settle there, work, and go to school until we left East Germany in 1949.

8

CHAPTER

What Happened, Father?

While we were living in Halle, Hannah Arendt, who then lived in New York, located us through the Red Cross. We received "America packages" of food that lifted us from the bare edge of survival to a measure of well-being. However, I had not forgotten starvation times or my love for life on the farm. These two factors combined with a religious fervor to "feed my sheep" and make my contribution of food to a starving world.

At age fifteen, newly arrived in West Germany, I began my farmwork apprenticeship. Without a farm to inherit, I followed the advice of elder friends and sought to immigrate to the United States. With Hannah Arendt's sponsorship, I succeeded and came to work on a dairy in California's Marin County. The dairy belonged to two Jewish families. Bill and Ellen Straus and Hans and Dina Angress and their children were friends of Hannah Arendt's. I was "the experimental German" there. And there again—now twenty-two years old—I encountered the truth of my recent German heritage and its effects on my employers' people "pulling no punches". Every one of my employers' friends who came to visit them on Blake's Landing Farms, their dairy, was the lone survivor of a large family. They had all been killed by the Germans—and I was the German there. Only because of my mother's status as victim had they accepted me as worker on their farm. My father's status, although known to Hannah Arendt, was not known to my employers. Father, I said truthfully, fought with an artillery unit in Russia, and at the Battle of the Bulge, and then again in Hungary, Austria, and Bavaria.

Although true enough to match the requirements of my employment, it was not the entire truth. The hidden portion of it burdened my mind very deeply and affected my work. After about a year of carrying that burden in a strange land, I remembered that upon my immigration, I had dutifully pledged to sign up for the draft. I decided to provide myself with a hiatus for my smitten German conscience. I asked the draft board to put me on top of the list—and soon I was training to be an American soldier.

Had I stayed in Germany, I would have resisted induction into the German army, newly joined into the NATO alliance. I remember coming back from a year as exchange student in Denmark in 1953 and visiting my father. I said, "So the father was pronounced a criminal for being a soldier? Shall I now join the soldiers to become a criminal by definition?"

Father said, "But if you are drafted, do everything the drill instructor tells you—or rather shouts at you." He told me what a lack of basic training can result in. During the Battle of the Bulge, some young kids were attached to the battery my father served with. They were under cover in a forest. The morning was crisp and cold, but the landscape was beautiful. One of the kids got out of his foxhole and walked toward the edge of the forest.

Dad and the other veterans yelled, "Down!"

It was too late. The boy was shot dead. I remembered that and benefitted from that advice during my basic training.

I was stationed in Germany—an American occupation soldier in the land of my father's glory and sin. The year was 1957. Some trouble in Iraq prompted President Eisenhower to send US armed forces to Lebanon. My unit, a transportation company, was sent to support a tank battalion that also went. In preparation for the event, our unit was sent to the NATO maneuver grounds of Bergen-Belsen. It was the area surrounding the site of the concentration camp where Anne Frank and thousands like her had been killed. Dina Angress, my American employer's wife, had almost ended up in that place. In Amsterdam, she—along with her parents and siblings—was waiting in line to be loaded onto German army trucks. The last truck was almost full. A soldier grabbed her and threw her on the truck before the gate was shut. Another soldier realized that Dina was the only member of her family on that truck. In a quick decision, he took her and threw her back down as the truck left.

We NATO soldiers were quartered in the onetime SS barracks at the end of the railway terminal. From there, it was a good half hour of a march to the camp, which was now a memorial sight. I requested and received a pass every evening of our unit's stay in that place, and I went to be alone in the memorial site. I would walk the gravel paths past the burial mounds. A sign in front of each announced the number of people buried there: six thousand, five thousand, eight thousand. The memorial ground is dominated by a memorial wall and an obelisk with the same inscription in many languages: "We shall never forget you."

The evening hours seemed so peaceful. In the daytime, there were rumblings of tanks, small arms, and artillery fire to be heard in the distance. But in the evening, all was quiet in the waning light. The wind in the birches and over the heather that covered the graves was the only sound. One Sunday, I was at the memorial site in the daytime. I was following a group of German people. One of the men commented on the inscriptions of the burial mounds as he passed them: "Anybody can write six thousand on a sign." Overhearing that comment, I understood that the devil never leaves human society; he only changes the clothes to suit the times and opportunities!

When I returned to the entrance gate, there was a unit of Dutch soldiers with their commanding officer. I saluted.

The officer returned the salute of the American soldier with his German conscience.

Along the path, close to the entrance, there were a number of individual memorial stones. I thought they were for people whose families might have been able to identify and bury them there individually.

A man wearing the skullcap of his Jewish faith was trying to take a photograph of one of the gravestones. The sun was against him, and he lacked a tripod, which might have helped him to shade the inscription on the stone while using the automatic camera release. As I walked by, he looked over and asked me to hold the cardboard for him. I did, and he thanked me. I asked him where he came from and if he had been there during the time it was a death camp.

He said he was from Amsterdam, and yes, he had been here.

I said, "It must have been horrible."

"Yes," said the man. He explained that the gravestones, including the one he had photographed, were only memorial stones put there by families. "The dead are all there," he said, pointing toward the burial mounds.

I asked if he had encountered any of his former guards.

He said no, but he also said that not all of them were all that demonic. "Some would have let us run away between the station and the camp, but where could we run to?"

I realized what he was saying. Anyone trying to run across the heather could easily have been picked off like a rabbit.

He thanked me once more and we parted. He said, "Look, let not the past wear you down. We must start something new now! We must go forward; don't turn back!" I nodded and knew that my American uniform had not deceived him. He looked right through it and into my soul, and on that day, my soul began to heal.

I asked Father how he had fared as a soldier in Hitler's SS. I also asked about the scenes other former soldiers had told me about. In Russia, entire villages had been driven together, forced to dig their own graves, and machine-gunned into the pit.

Father said he had been fortunate. As a member of a unit assigned to man a recoilless battery, he was never commanded to an extermination unit, but he was privy to those actions. He told me of one instance when the battery advanced into a small village. There were only women, children, and a few very old people. As they were setting up the battery and dispersing the vehicles into the fields, shots rang out. They all hit the dirt. When it was quiet again, a sizable number of his fellow soldiers were wounded or dead. "What are you going to do?" he asked, leaving me to ponder the choices.

When Father was drafted, he volunteered for training as a mountain ranger for ski patrolling. Two men on skis with full field packs and rifles would guide a fifty-caliber machine gun on a sled down a slope at full tilt. At a command, they had to be able to stop on the spot. Father was not athletic enough for that unit's demands, and he was transferred to a unit of automatic recoilless batteries. That unit was always put into the breach where the front was critically thin. They were continuously in Russia until 1944 when the unit was transferred to participate in Hitler's last offensive in the regions of the Ardennes. After the collapse of that offensive, the battery was transported eastward to Hungary. They crossed the Rhine River in Bonn, which was where Father and his family settled after the war—and where he and I went on long walks whenever I visited. He would talk, and I would listen. He and I were very close.

Father was called into staff headquarters, and his unit commander asked if he would like to become an officer.

Father begged off on medical grounds. Because of a slightly bent spine, he said, he was not athletic enough. He believed an officer could not ask his men to do what he himself could not perform. He said, "At that moment, I took notice of the athletic condition of those senior officers before me with their ample girth. And I thought, *Wilhelm, what did you just tell those guys?*"

The commanding officer's thin lips had the barest suggestion of a smile as he said, "All right, Jaensch. Dismissed!"

In Hungary, the day came when the battery was in retreat. They set up a defensive position. Father was forward observer as they came under heavy Russian bombardment from a battery the Germans called "the Stalin organ." Father's own battery fired a couple of shots, and then there was silence. Using a compass and his wits, he too made his retreat. He never did catch up with his unit again, but he reported to the nearest active unit in the field: an Austrian company of mountain rangers comprised of all kinds of German soldiers who all had lost their units. Father was appointed first sergeant of the company.

While he was with that unit, his company commander sent him up the hill on reconnaissance.

Father started out and had not walked very far when he felt some impact behind and below him. A machine gunner had spotted him and laid down a burst of machine-gun fire only inches behind and below him. Had he raised the muzzle of the gun even half an inch, Father would have been amputated. As a grenade exploded a little down the hill and behind him, he dived into the impact area and made his way downhill and back to his unit. He was able to report where the Russians were!

Jaensch Wilhelm and Fritz: father and son

The general retreat of the German forces had made every defensive position less and less tenable. Father had gotten through the entire war—until the beginning of 1945—without being wounded. One day, Father's unit got what German soldiers called a *Himmelfahrtskommando,* which is an assignment that is a sure way out of life. There was a factory with a wall and trenches running in front of the wall. The only retreat was sideways out of the trench. At the Russian advance, Father's unit accomplished that feat fairly well. Casualties were comparatively light. Father had gotten hit, but it was not a life-threatening injury. He was still able to help push a farm wagon with the more severely wounded soldiers to the rear.

Late in April 1945, Father was released from the hospital. He made his way toward the front in full SS combat uniform, not realizing there was no more front—and no unit in regular operation to report to. He stopped in a guesthouse to get something to eat. And there, around one of the tables, sat a group of freed concentration camp inmates. The men stared at him like the specter of a nightmare he must have been to them. He, in turn, realized that if the men decided to take action, he was done for. He sat down, ordered a meal, ate it, paid, and left.

Soon thereafter, he met a friendly couple on the highway. They told him the war was definitely over and suggested ridding himself at least of his insignia, which he did, feeling peculiarly strange and remiss of his soldier's duty. This report of my father's and similar observations about myself and other German people has led me to the theory that if there is anything typical about us Germans, then it is this: we have the tendency to live by permission. The Prussians in particular are rumored to be burdened with that need for an authority to tell them what to do. That, rather than some particularly vicious beastliness, has made Germans such a willing tool in the hands of their dictator.

Father was a loner all his life, and he was good at orienting himself in the field. So he had no trouble making his way northwestward toward the Ore Mountains since he knew his family was waiting. Near the Frankish town of Hof, he made the mistake of joining a group of ex-soldiers traveling in the same general direction. One ex-captain was a drag on the group because of his large knapsack, which was filled with loot. Generally, the men traveled only by night, avoiding highways and villages.

One day, they risked going through a village, and they were spotted by an American patrol. A farmhouse was built about a foot off the ground, and men dived under it. The captain couldn't get his knapsack under there, and the knapsack gave them away. All but a couple of the men surrendered right away. Father took a risk and stayed hidden, but when the patrol started firing under the farmhouse, he gave himself up too. He was fortunate by his own account. Had he been captured by the Russians, he would most likely not have lived.

In American custody, he was not treated with kid gloves, but in 1948, he was released to his family in Kasmark.

Fritz

The United States Army discharged me in 1958, and I returned to my farmwork. Some friends from the church I attended suggested that I go to school. So while continuing my farm work, managing Westminster Woods, the site for church retreats, farmwork again, and finally repair work and window cleaning––all while I attended school—I was able to earn BA and MA degrees. I was given the opportunity to finish all my coursework in the PhD program in history at UC Berkeley. Having run that ten-year course, I returned to my service work.

While studying at Sonoma State College (now Sonoma State University), I met Dr. John M. Steiner, a sociologist and Holocaust survivor. He shed some more light on my understanding of Father's military career. My mother was visiting at the time, and he said, "The man was fortunate. Had he been wounded earlier, chances are, he would have been sent to the concentration camps as a guard." Dr. Steiner knew of many such men who had guarded him in Auschwitz, Blechhammer, and Mauthausen.

When next I visited Father in Endenich, I told him what Dr. Steiner had said.

When Father heard Mauthausen, he said, "Yes, I was there. We stopped there whenever we came from the front, to get deloused and to receive a new issue of clothing. Upon reporting there, we were ordered to undress. Then we were led into a shower room—and there we were." He paused. "After showering we were reissued our clean uniforms. With mine on, I went out and did take a look at that operation." What astonished him, he said, and made him feel helpless in that situation was the frantic behavior of the guards and the haunted, exhausted specter of the prisoners they drove on.

Dr. Steiner's work was interviewing people like my father, all up and down the ranks of those who had once imprisoned him and hunted him like that. His work helped clarify what motivates people to join an organization like the SS and to what extent their participation is systemic circumstance or fate.

My father expressed an interest in and respect for Dr. Steiner's work. "When I was called up and sent to war, I was sworn in to fight for my country and to serve where I was commanded to serve."

A soldier's duty under fire. Who but a soldier understands that burden weighed in the scale of conscience?

I am blessed to have had three parents in Germany and a new home country in America, from where I was able to gain an understanding of my parents' trials during that perilous time filled with terrors.

As for me, I heed the word of the man I met in Belsen: "Remember well, but leave thoughts of fear and death behind. Turn forward instead to help build a future committed to life!"